Maps of the Environmental World

NATURAL-RESOURCE
MAPS

Jack and Meg Gillett

PowerKiDS
press.

New York

Published in 2013 by The Rosen Publishing Group, Inc.
29 East 21st Street, New York, NY 10010

Editor: Julia Adams
Designer: Rob Walster, Big Blu Design
Cover Design: Wayland
Map Art: Martin Sanders
Illustrations: Andy Stagg
Picture Research: Kathy Lockley/Julia Adams
Contributions by Richard and Louise Spilsbury

Picture Acknowledgments: All photography: Shutterstock, except: p. 10: Jack and Meg Gillett; p. 13, p. 24: iStock Images; p. 17: Paul Andrew Lawrence/Alamy

Library of Congress Cataloging-in-Publication Data

Gillett, Jack.
 Natural-resource maps / by Jack Gillett & Meg Gillett. — 1st ed.
    p. cm. — (Maps of the environmental world)
 Includes index.
 ISBN 978-1-4488-8612-8 (library binding) — ISBN 978-1-4488-8616-6 (pbk.) —
 ISBN 978-1-4488-8618-0 (6-pack)
 1. Natural resources—Juvenile literature. I. Gillett, Meg. II. Title.
 HC85.G55 2013
 333.7—dc23
                        2012004335

Manufactured in the United States of America

CPSIA Compliance Information: Batch #B4S12PK: For Further Information contact Rosen Publishing, New York, New York at 1-800-237-9932

Contents

Introduction

This book looks at the natural resources that are found and used around the world. These include essentials, such as water and food, but also natural resources such as metals that make bicycles, cell phones and other things that we enjoy having, but can live without.

The location of a country determines what natural resources it has and the distribution of these resources affect a country's development. For example, some countries with plenty of mineral resources have developed industries that turn those minerals into products.

Globe shows the location of the map region

Fun research activity

Pictures highlight features discussed or located on the map

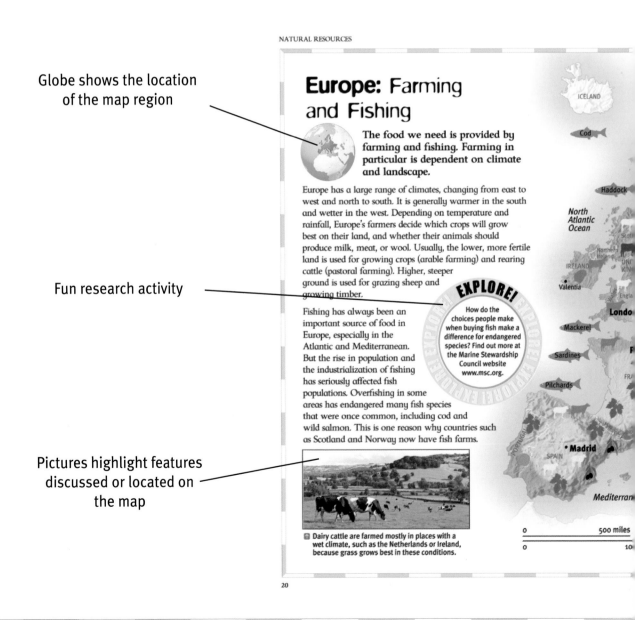

NATURAL RESOURCES

Europe: Farming and Fishing

The food we need is provided by farming and fishing. Farming in particular is dependent on climate and landscape.

Europe has a large range of climates, changing from east to west and north to south. It is generally warmer in the south and wetter in the west. Depending on temperature and rainfall, Europe's farmers decide which crops will grow best on their land, and whether their animals should produce milk, meat, or wool. Usually, the lower, more fertile land is used for growing crops (arable farming) and rearing cattle (pastoral farming). Higher, steeper ground is used for grazing sheep and growing timber.

Fishing has always been an important source of food in Europe, especially in the Atlantic and Mediterranean. But the rise in population and the industrialization of fishing has seriously affected fish populations. Overfishing in some areas has endangered many fish species that were once common, including cod and wild salmon. This is one reason why countries such as Scotland and Norway now have fish farms.

EXPLORE!
How do the choices people make when buying fish make a difference for endangered species? Find out more at the Marine Stewardship Council website www.msc.org.

Dairy cattle are farmed mostly in places with a wet climate, such as the Netherlands or Ireland, because grass grows best in these conditions.

ICELAND · Cod · Haddock · North Atlantic Ocean · IRELAND · Valentia · Mackerel · Sardines · Pilchards · London · Madrid · SPAIN · Mediterran

0   500 miles

20

There is a limited amount of most of the Earth's natural resources and one day they will run out. Digging up or obtaining these resources can damage or destroy habitats. Also, processing raw materials into products uses large amounts of energy, which causes pollution and contributes to climate change. In the future, it will become increasingly important to find alternative ways of sourcing natural resources, such as recycling.

Each double page in this book introduces the location and distribution of natural resources in a different region of the world. A map locates relevant sites and graphs, and statistics provide important data. At the end of the book is a section you can use for further study and comparisons.

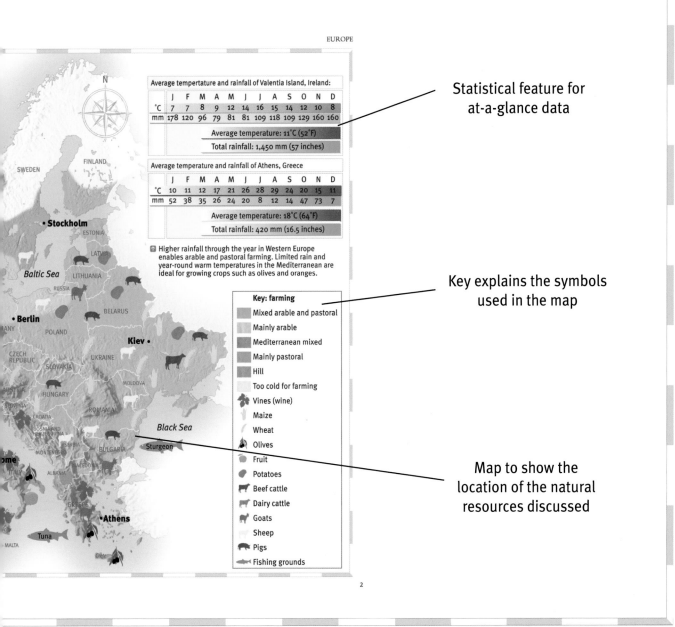

EUROPE

Average temperature and rainfall of Valentia Island, Ireland:

	J	F	M	A	M	J	J	A	S	O	N	D
°C	7	7	8	9	12	14	16	15	14	12	10	8
mm	178	120	96	79	81	81	109	118	109	129	160	160

Average temperature: 11°C (52°F)

Total rainfall: 1,450 mm (57 inches)

Average temperature and rainfall of Athens, Greece

	J	F	M	A	M	J	J	A	S	O	N	D
°C	10	11	12	17	21	26	28	29	24	20	15	11
mm	52	38	35	26	24	20	8	12	14	47	73	7

Average temperature: 18°C (64°F)

Total rainfall: 420 mm (16.5 inches)

Higher rainfall through the year in Western Europe enables arable and pastoral farming. Limited rain and year-round warm temperatures in the Mediterranean are ideal for growing crops such as olives and oranges.

Key: farming

- Mixed arable and pastoral
- Mainly arable
- Mediterranean mixed
- Mainly pastoral
- Hill
- Too cold for farming
- Vines (wine)
- Maize
- Wheat
- Olives
- Fruit
- Potatoes
- Beef cattle
- Dairy cattle
- Goats
- Sheep
- Pigs
- Fishing grounds

SWEDEN, FINLAND, ESTONIA, LATVIA, LITHUANIA, RUSSIA, BELARUS, POLAND, UKRAINE, MOLDOVA, CZECH REPUBLIC, SLOVAKIA, HUNGARY, AUSTRIA, SLOVENIA, CROATIA, ROMANIA, BOSNIA AND HERZEGOVINA, SERBIA, MONTENEGRO, BULGARIA, MACEDONIA, ALBANIA, GREECE, ITALY, MALTA

Stockholm, Berlin, Kiev, Athens

Baltic Sea, Black Sea

Sturgeon, Tuna, Tuna

Statistical feature for at-a-glance data

Key explains the symbols used in the map

Map to show the location of the natural resources discussed

2

The World: Water Supply

Water is an essential natural resource. People can survive for three weeks without food, but may die after three days without water. We need water to live, to cook, keep clean, grow crops, and raise livestock. People also use water for nonessential purposes. Industrialized countries use vast amounts of water in factories and power stations, and in things like washing machines and swimming pools.

There is a limited, or finite, amount of water on Earth and people in different locations have a different share of it. Water availability is mainly affected by climate. Places with hot, dry climates, such as deserts, have little rainfall. Places with rainy seasons have more water and can store surplus water in reservoirs. In some places water is polluted and cannot be safely used by people without expensive treatment. With a rising global population, and increasing nonessential water use, supplying enough water for everyone is a major challenge in the twenty-first century.

NORTH AMERICA

Mojave Desert

Sonoran Desert

SOUTH AMERICA

Atacama Desert

Monte Desert

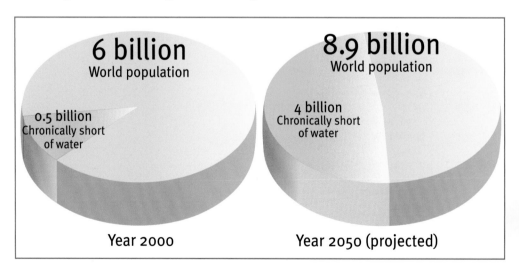

6 billion
World population

0.5 billion
Chronically short
of water

Year 2000

8.9 billion
World population

4 billion
Chronically short
of water

Year 2050 (projected)

⬆ By 2050, experts predict that nearly half the world's population will have a chronic water shortage. This means they will not have enough to remain healthy.

N

ASIA

EUROPE

Gobi Desert

EXPLORE!

Think of all
the ways in which
you use water. Which
of these are essential,
and which are
nonessential?

Thar
Desert

Sahara

Arabian
Desert

AFRICA

Great
Sandy
Desert

AUSTRALIA

Great
Victoria
Desert

Kalahari
Desert

Key

Areas that usually have a water surplus

Areas that are chronically short of water

The World: Fossil Fuels

Coal, gas, and oil are natural resources that we call fossil fuels. They formed from the remains of plants and animals that lived millions of years ago. We mostly use these resources to generate useful energy.

Coal is mostly burned in power stations to generate electricity. Gas is also used in power stations, as well as being piped into homes to use for heating and cooking. Gasoline and diesel made from oil are essential to make the engines in cars, airplanes, and ships work. We use enormous amounts of energy and this is rising each year because of the growing world population and increased use of vehicles and electricity in modern life.

Some countries have more fossil fuel reserves than others, but all fossil fuels will run out one day. Another problem is that burning fossil fuels causes pollution. This is why people are looking for alternative, sustainable energy resources, such as water, wind, and solar (Sun) power.

Greenland

Alaska
(US)

Canada

NORTH AMERICA

United States

Mexico

Venezuela

Colombia

Ecuador

SOUTH
AMERICA

Peru

Brazil

Bolivia

Paraguay

Chile

Argentina

Uruguay

Years

300
250
200
150
100
50
0

Coal
Gas
Oil

⬆ This bar graph shows about how many years we can still use each fossil fuel.

⬆ Oil refineries changes crude oil from under the ground into fuels and many other by-products, such as plastics.

N

Iceland

Norway
Sweden
Finland

Russia

ASIA

UK

EUROPE

Ukraine

Kazakhstan

Mongolia

France

Japan

Spain

Turkey

China

Morocco

Iraq Iran

Pakistan

Algeria Libya Egypt

Saudi
Arabia

India

Mali

Niger

Chad Sudan

Thailand

Nigeria

Malaysia

AFRICA

Ethiopia

Dem.
Repub.
of Congo

Indonesia

Papua
New
Guinea

Angola

Zambia

Madagascar

Namibia

Australia

South
Africa

AUSTRALIA

New
Zealand

Antarctica

Key

	Oil field
	Coalfield
	Gas field

EXPLORE!

Find out
which of the three
fossil fuels pollutes
the air the most.
Which pollutes the
air the least?

Europe: Metallic Minerals

Metallic minerals are natural substances from the Earth from which we get metals such as copper and iron. These metals are used to produce many of the things we use in everyday life, including airplanes, bridges, and computers.

Different amounts and types of metals are found in rocks called ores in different locations worldwide. The Industrial Revolution began in Europe because of the metallic minerals there. The region also had fossil fuels to power machines and factories that turned the raw materials into useful things, such as ships and railways.

There is a limited supply of metallic minerals and they are being used up as people buy more and develop new metal products. For example, silver, used for electronics and jewelry, could run out by 2020. We can recycle some metals by melting and reusing them. It takes 5 tons (4.5 t) of bauxite ore to make 1 ton (.9 t) of new aluminum, but none to make recycled aluminum.

⬆ This steelworks in Sheffield, UK, uses iron ore found nearby to make steel, and local coal to power its machines.

EXPLORE!

Find out which metallic minerals are used to produce the following products: cell phone, car, computer, and fridge.

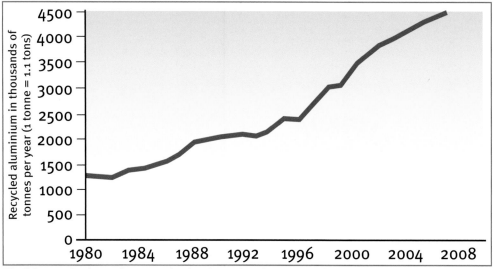

⬆ This graph shows how much aluminum has been recycled in Europe since 1980. The amount is increasing, currently reaching around 90 percent of drinks cans. Today, Europe is a global leader in recycling metals, along with North America and Japan.

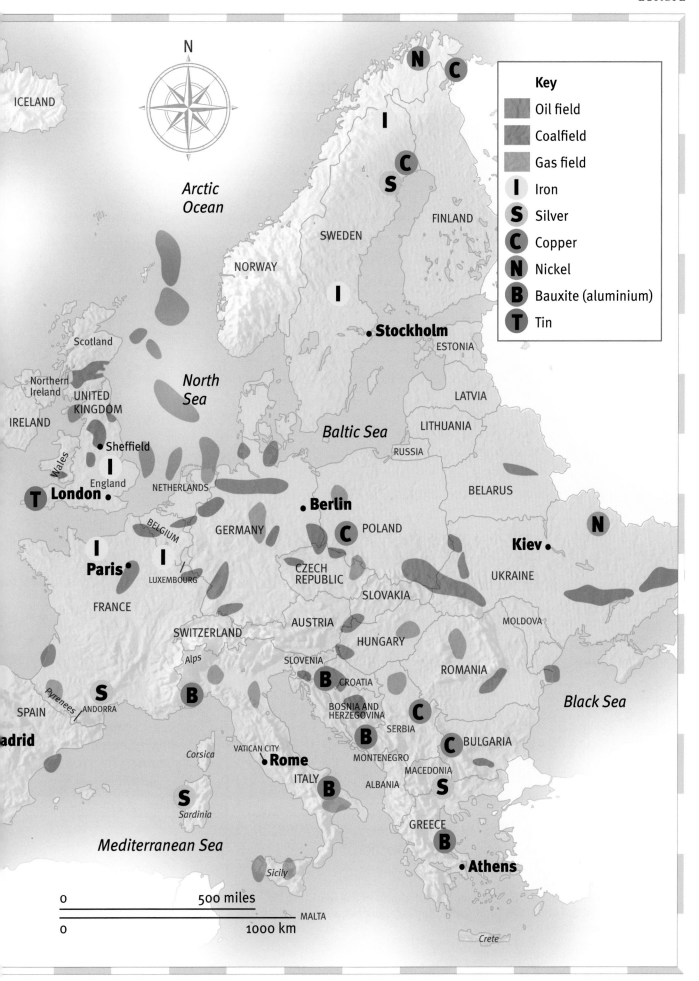

N

Arctic
Ocean

ICELAND

N C

I

C
S

SWEDEN

FINLAND

NORWAY

Stockholm

ESTONIA

North
Sea

Baltic Sea

LATVIA

LITHUANIA

Scotland

RUSSIA

Northern
Ireland

UNITED
KINGDOM

I

Sheffield

BELARUS

IRELAND

Wales

England

T **London**

NETHERLANDS

Berlin

N

BELGIUM

C

POLAND

Kiev

I **Paris**

I

GERMANY

LUXEMBOURG

CZECH
REPUBLIC

UKRAINE

FRANCE

SLOVAKIA

SWITZERLAND

AUSTRIA

MOLDOVA

Alps

HUNGARY

SLOVENIA

B

CROATIA

ROMANIA

S

BOSNIA AND
HERZEGOVINA

C

Black Sea

SPAIN

ANDORRA

Pyrenees

B

SERBIA

adrid

Corsica

VATICAN CITY

Rome

B

MONTENEGRO

C

BULGARIA

ITALY

ALBANIA

S

S

Sardinia

MACEDONIA

B

GREECE

Mediterranean Sea

B

Athens

Sicily

Key	
	Oil field
	Coalfield
	Gas field
I	Iron
S	Silver
C	Copper
N	Nickel
B	Bauxite (aluminium)
T	Tin

0   500 miles

MALTA

0   1000 km

Crete

Africa: Precious Metals and Stones

Precious metals and stones are rare and valuable minerals. Apart from jewelry, these natural resources are used in other ways, too. For example, hard diamonds are used to make cutting and drilling tools and gold is used in electronics.

Africa is rich in precious stones and metals. South Africa has large amounts of gold and diamonds. Like metallic minerals, most of these precious minerals have to be mined and dug out from under the ground, causing environmental damage.

Some parts of Africa are able to grow food and other crops such as cotton, but generally farming is difficult because of the hot and dry climate. In fact, deserts are spreading, mainly due to climate change, causing hardship in drier regions. This is why a lot of African countries are so reliant on the trade and export of precious metals and stones.

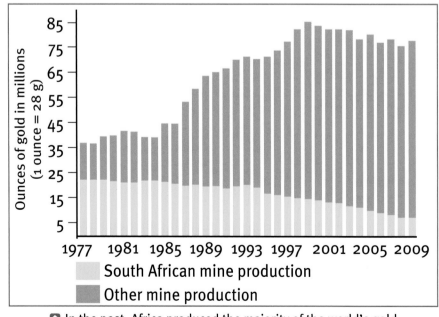

⬆ In the past, Africa produced the majority of the world's gold, but the amount it produces today is falling because supplies are running out.

EXPLORE!

Which African countries produce tantalum? What is it used for and why is demand growing?

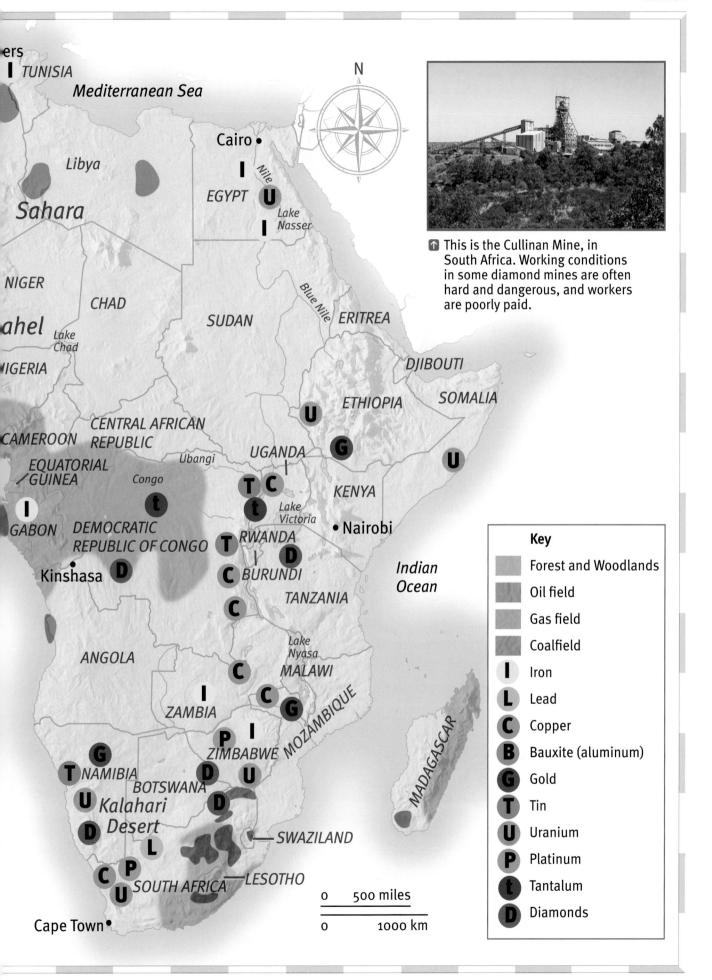

TUNISIA

Mediterranean Sea

Cairo •

N

Libya

EGYPT

Nile

Lake Nasser

Sahara

NIGER

CHAD

SUDAN

Blue Nile

ERITREA

⬆ This is the Cullinan Mine, in South Africa. Working conditions in some diamond mines are often hard and dangerous, and workers are poorly paid.

ahel

Lake Chad

IGERIA

DJIBOUTI

CENTRAL AFRICAN REPUBLIC

Ubangi

UGANDA

ETHIOPIA

SOMALIA

CAMEROON

EQUATORIAL GUINEA

Congo

KENYA

GABON

DEMOCRATIC REPUBLIC OF CONGO

RWANDA

Lake Victoria

• Nairobi

Kinshasa •

BURUNDI

Indian Ocean

TANZANIA

Lake Nyasa

MALAWI

Key

	Forest and Woodlands
	Oil field
	Gas field
	Coalfield

ANGOLA

ZAMBIA

MOZAMBIQUE

MADAGASCAR

NAMIBIA

ZIMBABWE

BOTSWANA

Kalahari Desert

SWAZILAND

LESOTHO

SOUTH AFRICA

Cape Town •

o   500 miles

o   1000 km

I Iron
L Lead
C Copper
B Bauxite (aluminum)
G Gold
T Tin
U Uranium
P Platinum
t Tantalum
D Diamonds

North America: Industrial Raw Materials

Industrial raw materials are resources such as metals and fuels that are used to make products in factories. These are then sold within a country or exported. For example, lead is used to make batteries, and oil can be used to make plastic.

North America contains many industrial raw materials. It also has the fossil fuels needed to extract those resources and to power the factories that turn them into products. Having plentiful natural resources has helped to make the United States the richest nation in the world, and Canada one of the world's More Economically Developed Countries (MEDCs).

Among North America's big industries are car manufacturers Ford, Chrysler, and General Motors, aircraft builder Boeing, and Microsoft, which is a world leader in computer technology. Canada has a smaller population than the United States, and its wealth comes more from extracting and exporting raw materials.

◀ Many of Canada's copper, iron ore, and uranium mines are in its frozen, northern, wilderness area. This is an iron ore mine in Labrador.

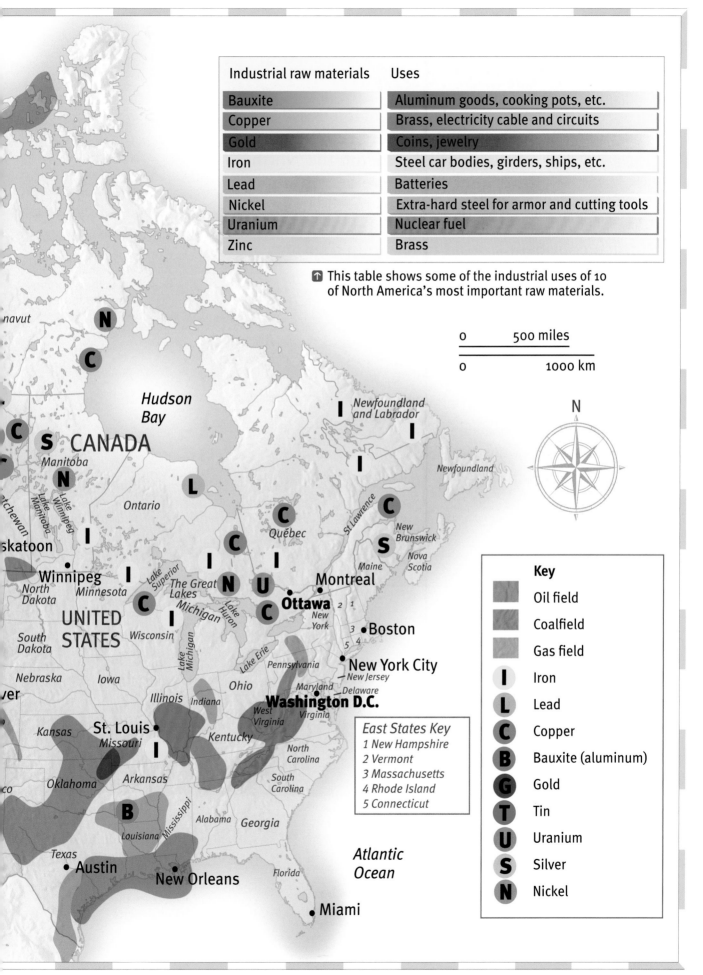

Industrial raw materials	Uses
Bauxite	Aluminum goods, cooking pots, etc.
Copper	Brass, electricity cable and circuits
Gold	Coins, jewelry
Iron	Steel car bodies, girders, ships, etc.
Lead	Batteries
Nickel	Extra-hard steel for armor and cutting tools
Uranium	Nuclear fuel
Zinc	Brass

⬆ This table shows some of the industrial uses of 10 of North America's most important raw materials.

0   500 miles

0   1000 km

N

Hudson Bay

Nunavut

CANADA

Manitoba

Ontario

Québec

Newfoundland and Labrador

Newfoundland

St Lawrence

New Brunswick

Nova Scotia

Maine

Montreal

Ottawa

New York

Boston

New York City

New Jersey

Washington D.C.

Winnipeg

North Dakota

Minnesota

Lake Superior

The Great Lakes

Lake Michigan

Lake Huron

Lake Erie

Wisconsin

UNITED STATES

South Dakota

Nebraska

Iowa

Illinois

Indiana

Ohio

Pennsylvania

Maryland

Delaware

West Virginia

Virginia

Kansas

Missouri

St. Louis

Kentucky

North Carolina

South Carolina

Oklahoma

Arkansas

Alabama

Georgia

Mississippi

Louisiana

Texas

Austin

New Orleans

Florida

Miami

Atlantic Ocean

skatoon

chewan

ver

co

East States Key
1 New Hampshire
2 Vermont
3 Massachusetts
4 Rhode Island
5 Connecticut

Key
▨	Oil field
▨	Coalfield
▨	Gas field
I	Iron
L	Lead
C	Copper
B	Bauxite (aluminum)
G	Gold
T	Tin
U	Uranium
S	Silver
N	Nickel

The Poles: Gas and Oil

As amounts of available fossil fuels diminish, more remote parts of the world, including the North and South Poles, are becoming more important as providers of these resources. Antarctica is an icy continent so cold and windy that few people live there except research scientists.

Antarctic waters are rich in fish and other animals that many penguins and whales feed on. Oil and gas are mostly found deep underwater where exploration and drilling are risky. They need to be carefully and sustainably carried out to avoid pollution and coastal damage affecting ocean wildlife.

The ocean surrounding Antarctica is very rich in marine life. Killing whales there for food is illegal, but some countries still do it even though it endangers the whale population.

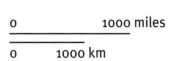

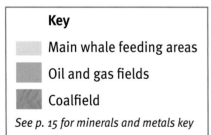

Key

Main whale feeding areas

Oil and gas fields

Coalfield

See p. 15 for minerals and metals key

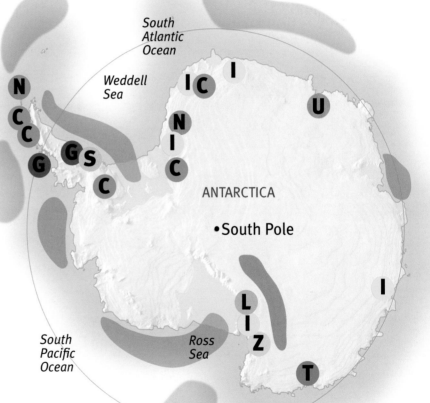

Average South Pole temperature and precipitation by month:

	J	F	M	A	M	J	J	A	S	O	N	D
°C	-32	-44	-58	-65	-66	-65	-68	-69	-66	-57	-32	-55
mm	0.1	0	0.7	0.5	0.4	0.5	0.6	0.7	0.3	0.2	0.1	0

Average temperature: -60°C (-76°F)

Total precipitation: 4 mm (0.16 inch)

Antarctica has the world's coldest temperatures but strong winds make it feel even colder! Rain falls as snow around the coast, but central places such as the South Pole are as dry as deserts.

The Arctic is a region of frozen ocean surrounded by the coldest parts of Asia, Europe, and North America.

Arctic oil and gas reserves have been drilled mostly on these continents. Any oil spills from pipes and tankers take longer to naturally clear away in cold waters. Therefore, Arctic pollution can stick around for a long time.

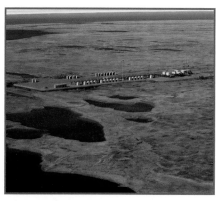

⬆ Coastal Alaska has some of the United States' richest oil fields. With global warming, oil companies will be able to drill further out into the Arctic Ocean because less of its surface is freezing over each year.

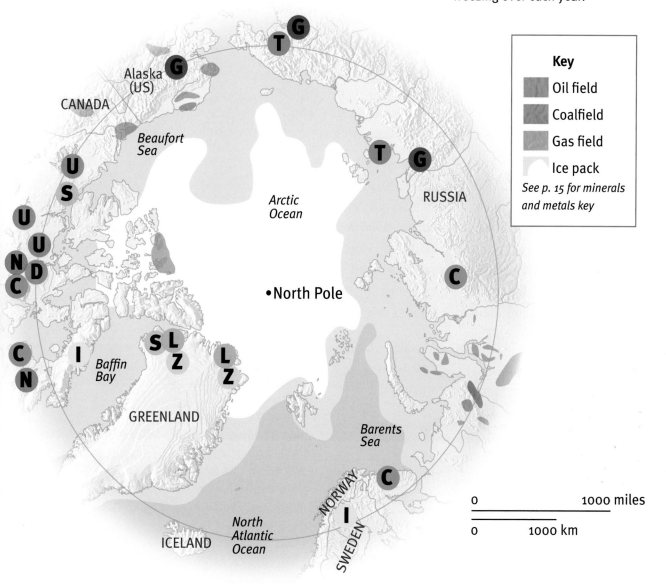

Key

- Oil field
- Coalfield
- Gas field
- Ice pack

See p. 15 for minerals and metals key

CANADA
Alaska (US)
Beaufort Sea
Arctic Ocean
•North Pole
RUSSIA
Baffin Bay
GREENLAND
Barents Sea
NORWAY
SWEDEN
North Atlantic Ocean
ICELAND

0   1000 miles
0   1000 km

The World: Forests and Forest Products

We need wood for construction, paper, cardboard, musical instruments, and many other products. People harvest wood from naturally growing forests and from plantations.

Hardwoods, used to make plywood and furniture, come from slow-growing trees. These include mahogany and teak, which grow in humid tropical rain forests, and oak and beech from cooler deciduous woodland. Fast-growing coniferous trees such as spruce and pine grow best in cold climates. Large areas of forest worldwide are being chopped down to meet the rising demand for timber. This is called deforestation.

Wood is not a finite resource, but trees take years, decades, or, in the case of some hardwoods, centuries to grow. People are not using this resource sustainably and land is deforested quicker than it is replanted. Deforestation also affects the atmosphere. Trees use up carbon dioxide to make the oxygen most living things need to breathe. With fewer trees, there is less oxygen and more carbon dioxide that traps heat, causing global warming.

Greenland

Alaska (US)

Canada

NORTH AMERICA

United States

Mexico

Venezuela

Colombia

Ecuador

Peru

SOUTH AMERICA

Brazil

Bolivia

Paraguay

Chile

Argentina

Uruguay

⬆ These rain forest mahogany trees took over a hundred years to grow. Their hardwood can be used to make expensive furniture.

EXPLORE!
Every year, 0.2 percent of the world's forests are chopped down and not replaced. At this rate of deforestation, how many years will our forests last?

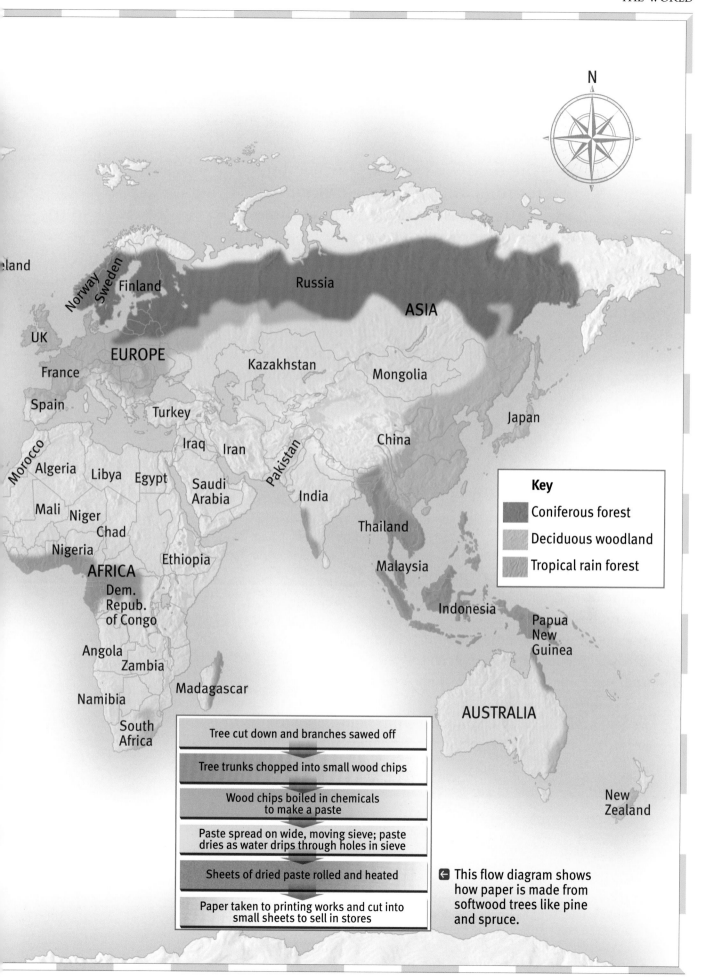

N

eland

Norway
Sweden
Finland
Russia
ASIA

UK

EUROPE
Kazakhstan
Mongolia

France
Japan

Spain
Turkey
China

Morocco
Iraq
Iran
Pakistan

Algeria
Libya
Egypt
Saudi
Arabia
India

Mali
Niger
Chad
Thailand

Nigeria
Ethiopia
Malaysia

AFRICA
Dem.
Repub.
of Congo
Indonesia
Papua
New
Guinea

Angola
Zambia

Namibia
Madagascar

South
Africa
AUSTRALIA

New
Zealand

Key

Coniferous forest

Deciduous woodland

Tropical rain forest

Tree cut down and branches sawed off

Tree trunks chopped into small wood chips

Wood chips boiled in chemicals
to make a paste

Paste spread on wide, moving sieve; paste
dries as water drips through holes in sieve

Sheets of dried paste rolled and heated

Paper taken to printing works and cut into
small sheets to sell in stores

← This flow diagram shows
how paper is made from
softwood trees like pine
and spruce.

Europe: Farming and Fishing

The food we need is provided by farming and fishing. Farming in particular is dependent on climate and landscape.

Europe has a large range of climates, changing from east to west and north to south. It is generally warmer in the south and wetter in the west. Depending on temperature and rainfall, Europe's farmers decide which crops will grow best on their land, and whether their animals should produce milk, meat, or wool. Usually, the lower, more fertile land is used for growing crops (arable farming) and rearing cattle (pastoral farming). Higher, steeper ground is used for grazing sheep and growing timber.

Fishing has always been an important source of food in Europe, especially in the Atlantic and Mediterranean. But the rise in population and the industrialization of fishing has seriously affected fish populations. Overfishing in some areas has endangered many fish species that were once common, including cod and wild salmon. This is one reason why countries such as Scotland and Norway now have fish farms.

EXPLORE!

How do the choices people make when buying fish make a difference for endangered species? Find out more at the Marine Stewardship Council website www.msc.org.

⬆ Dairy cattle are farmed mostly in places with a wet climate, such as the Netherlands or Ireland, because grass grows best in these conditions.

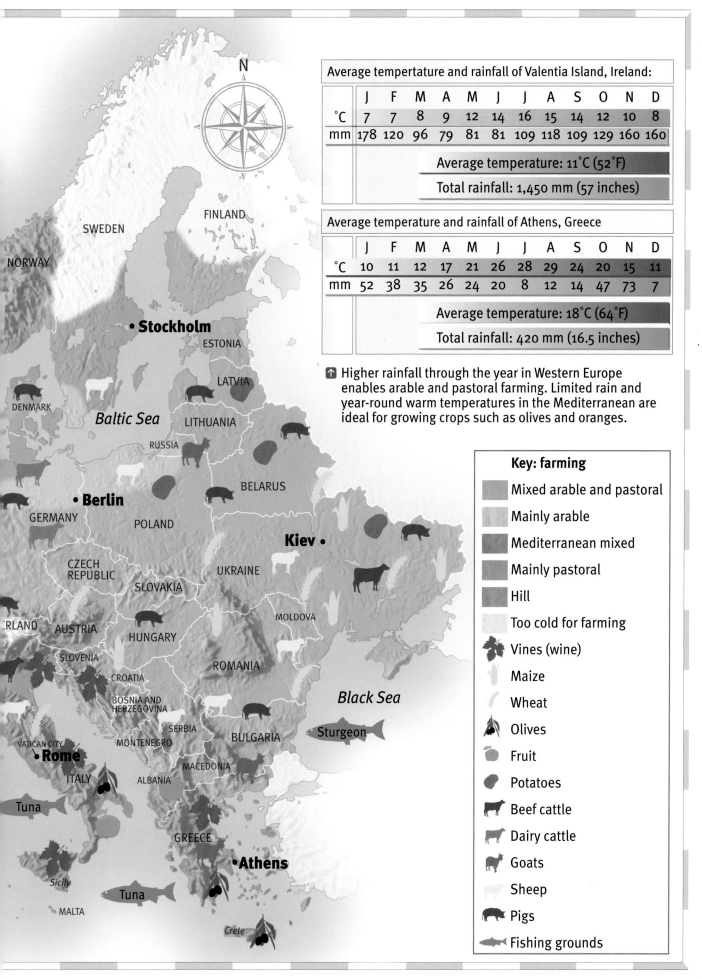

Average temperature and rainfall of Valentia Island, Ireland:

	J	F	M	A	M	J	J	A	S	O	N	D
°C	7	7	8	9	12	14	16	15	14	12	10	8
mm	178	120	96	79	81	81	109	118	109	129	160	160

Average temperature: 11°C (52°F)

Total rainfall: 1,450 mm (57 inches)

Average temperature and rainfall of Athens, Greece

	J	F	M	A	M	J	J	A	S	O	N	D
°C	10	11	12	17	21	26	28	29	24	20	15	11
mm	52	38	35	26	24	20	8	12	14	47	73	7

Average temperature: 18°C (64°F)

Total rainfall: 420 mm (16.5 inches)

⬆ Higher rainfall through the year in Western Europe enables arable and pastoral farming. Limited rain and year-round warm temperatures in the Mediterranean are ideal for growing crops such as olives and oranges.

Key: farming

- Mixed arable and pastoral
- Mainly arable
- Mediterranean mixed
- Mainly pastoral
- Hill
- Too cold for farming
- Vines (wine)
- Maize
- Wheat
- Olives
- Fruit
- Potatoes
- Beef cattle
- Dairy cattle
- Goats
- Sheep
- Pigs
- Fishing grounds

NORWAY
SWEDEN
FINLAND
Stockholm
ESTONIA
LATVIA
DENMARK
Baltic Sea
LITHUANIA
RUSSIA
BELARUS
Berlin
GERMANY
POLAND
Kiev
CZECH REPUBLIC
SLOVAKIA
UKRAINE
RLAND
AUSTRIA
HUNGARY
MOLDOVA
SLOVENIA
CROATIA
ROMANIA
Black Sea
BOSNIA AND HERZEGOVINA
SERBIA
Sturgeon
MONTENEGRO
BULGARIA
VATICAN CITY
Rome
MACEDONIA
ITALY
ALBANIA
Tuna
GREECE
Athens
Sicily
Tuna
MALTA
Crete

Southeast Asia:
Monoculture

Monoculture farming is growing a single crop, such as palm oil, over a wide area. In Southeast Asia the main monoculture crops in many countries are rice and rubber.

Rice is a staple food in Southeast Asia. It is the main part of the diet for most people. Southeast Asia has warm temperatures and plentiful rain to keep rice roots wet, which are ideal conditions for growing large amounts of rice. Rice is farmed in flat valleys but also on small terraces cut into mountainsides, with mud walls to trap rainwater. Around 75 percent of global rice production is in Southeast Asia, and China is the major world producer.

Rubber trees are widely grown on large plantations in Southeast Asia. A milky liquid called latex containing rubber is produced under the tree bark. The latex is collected and processed into solid rubber for making tires and other products including hoses and surgical gloves. Indonesia, Malaysia, and Thailand together produce 72 percent of the world's natural rubber.

Monocultures have low biodiversity. Agricultural chemicals to clear weeds and pests from crops harm wildlife, remove their habitat, and pollute water. One example of sustainable monoculture farming in Southeast Asia is keeping fish in paddies to eat rice pests without using chemicals. Farmers can eat or sell the fish, too.

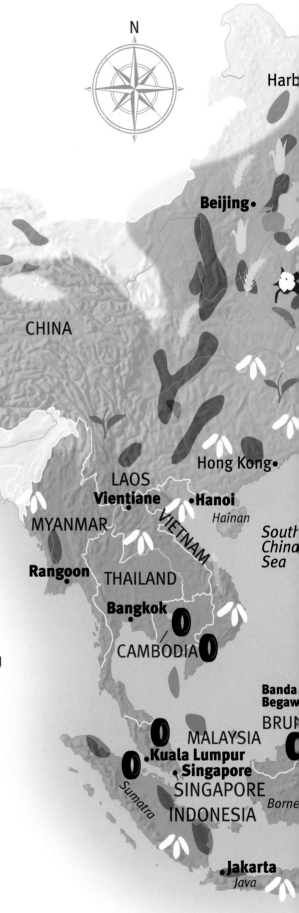

Key

- Oil field
- Coalfield
- Gas field
- Deciduous woodland
- Tropical rain forest
- Mountains
- Rice
- Rubber
- Wheat
- Maize
- Fruit
- Cotton
- Cocoa
- Sugar
- Tea

⬆ Cups attached to these rubber trees in a Malaysian plantation collect the latex sap oozing from spiral cuts in the bark.

EXPLORE!

Around half of all rubber used does not come from trees, but instead is manmade. Which natural resources is synthetic rubber made from and where are they produced?

Pacific Ocean

PAPUA NEW GUINEA

New Guinea

• **Port Moresby**

Celebes

0		500 miles
0	500 km	

•**Dili**

EAST TIMOR

⬆ Extra rice fields have been made in Bali, Indonesia, by making terraces on steep hillsides.

Brazil: Forest and Farmland

Brazil is the leading world producer not only of oranges and coffee, grown in the southeast, but also beef and soy beans, farmed in the center of the country. However, around 60 percent of Brazil is covered with thick rain forest.

The Brazilian meat industry has grown rapidly over the last 20 years because it exports cheap beef around the world. Today it has over 200 million livestock. Export demand for soy beans, mostly as livestock feed but also for human consumption, is also rising in some areas.

As Brazil increases its export, farmland is created by deforestation. Mostly, the deforested areas are used for cattle ranching. Between 1996 and 2006 an area of pasture the size of Portugal was created by deforestation. Most Brazilian soy is farmed in cleared grassland, but farmers forced off this land then clear new farmland in the rain forest.

Brazil supplies 39 percent of the total world soy bean exports, largely to China and Europe. As the world population grows, so will export demand for meat and soy, driving further deforestation.

Rio Negro
Rio Japurá
Amazon
Rio Juruá
Amazon Basin
Porto Ve
Rio Purus
Rio Branco•
Chapada
Pareci

EXPLORE!
Use the Internet to find out how much soy is exported via the ports of Paranaguá and Santos. Where is it exported to?

⬆ A herd of Brazilian cattle, called Zebu, graze on newly deforested ground in the Amazon Basin. The edge of the rain forest is visible in the background.

Brazil's yearly deforested area in km² (1 km² = 247 acres)

| | 30,000 |
| 20,000 |
| 10,000 |
| 0% |

1990 | 1995 | 2000 | 2005 | 2010

Years

⬆ In some years, the rate of deforestation in Brazil is over three times greater than the world as a whole.

Boa Vista

Amazon Basin

Rio Trombetas

Rio Jari

Rio Paru

•Macapá

Amazon

•Belém

•Manaus

•Santarém

•São Luís

•Fortaleza

Rio Tapajós

Rio Iriri

Rio Xingu

Rio Tocantins

•Teresina

•Natal

Rio Parnaíba

Juazeiro do Norte •

•João
Pessoa

Campina Grande •

•Recife

•Maceió

quemes

Teles Pires

BRAZIL

Serra dos Gradas

Rio São Francisco

•Paluas do
Tocantins

Salvador

•Cuiabá

Rio Jequitinhonha

•Rondonópolis

•Brasília

•Goiânia

Brazilian Highlands

Rio Grande

Campo•
Grande

Rio Paraná

•Belo Horizonte

•Vitória

Rio Paranapanema

Campinas

Rio Ivaí

São Paulo•

Rio de Janeiro

Santos

Curitiba

Rio Iguaçu

•Paranaguá

•Florianopólis

•Passo Fundo

Santa Maria

•Porto Alegre

•Rio Grande

0   500 miles

0   1000 km

Key	
	Tropical rain forest
	Deforestation
	Sugar cane
	Coastal woodland
	Oil field
	Coalfield
	Soy beans
	Rubber
	Maize
	Coffee
	Cocoa
	Fruit
	Cotton
	Beef cattle

North America:
Extensive Farming

In North America most arable or crop farming happens in the Great Plains. This region is the world's largest producer of wheat.

The Great Plains were first used for arable farming because they have warm summers and adequate rainfall, and soil that retains moisture. They are also flat enough to use big machines to farm large areas extensively. Today arable farming in North America is big business. It is becoming more intensive, and requires more chemical fertilizers and pesticides to grow sufficient crops in the plains than in the past. This is due to huge amounts of crops depleting the minerals in the soil.

The growing world population needs more food and North America has little spare crop land to grow more. It is increasing productivity by using genetically modified, or GM, crops. These are crops such as corn or soy beans grown from special seeds with certain changed or modified genes. This makes the crops, for example, produce more food per plant or resist crop pests. North America produces nearly 70 percent of the world's combined GM crop weight.

Alaska (US)

Anchorage •

San
Franc

⬆ This machine harvests wheat in the state of Washington. Wheat fields in the United States cover about 60 million acres (24.2 million ha) of land.

EXPLORE!

Using genetically modified crops is a controversial issue. What are the advantages and disadvantages of growing GM crops?

Key

Coniferous forest

Mixed farming

Arable farming, the Great Plains

Pastoral farming

Hot desert

Ice desert

Vegetable growing on irrigated farmland

See p. 21 for crop and animal symbols key

Arctic Ocean

Great Bear Lake

Northwest Territories

Great Slave Lake

Nunavut

Hudson Bay

Lake Athabasca

Labrador

Newfoundland and Labrador

CANADA

Alberta

Saskatchewan

Manitoba

Lake Manitoba

Lake Winnipeg

Ontario

Québec

Newfoundland

Edmonton

Saskatoon

Winnipeg

St. Lawrence

New Brunswick

Grand Banks

Nova Scotia

Cod

ish umbia

ncouver

attle

gton

Montana

North Dakota

Minnesota

Lake Superior

The Great Lakes

Michigan

Lake Huron

Montréal

Maine

Herring

Hake

Idaho

Wisconsin

Lake Michigan

Ottawa

New York

Toronto

Boston

nento

nda

Wyoming

South Dakota

USA

Lake Erie

New York City

New Jersey

Las Vegas

Utah

Colorado

Nebraska

Iowa

Chicago

Indiana

Ohio

Pennsylvania

Washington D.C.

Maryland

Delaware

Rocky Mountains

Denver

Kansas

St. Louis

Illinois

Missouri

Kentucky

West Virginia

Virginia

East States Key
1 New Hampshire
2 Vermont
3 Massachusetts
4 Rhode Island
5 Connecticut

ria

les

Arizona

Phoenix

New Mexico

Oklahoma

Arkansas

Tennessee

North Carolina

South Carolina

North Atlantic Ocean

Texas

Mississippi

Alabama

Georgia

Louisiana

Austin

New Orleans

Florida

Miami

Gulf of Mexico

| 0 | 500 miles |
| 0 | 1000 km |

Australia: Irrigation Farming

Australia is one of the world's driest countries. Two thirds of its area is classed as arid, with insufficient rainfall for plants to grow, and much of this is barren desert. The hot, arid interior of Australia is only suitable for rearing sheep and cattle where farmers can irrigate the land.

Crops including wheat, barley, sorghum, and cotton mostly grow in wetter New South Wales and Victoria, but big, regular harvests can only be guaranteed in most areas using irrigation from both rivers and groundwater. Digging ever deeper for sufficient groundwater is causing widespread salination in Australia. This is when underground salts come to the surface making soil useless for crops or pasture.

When soil damaged by salination, livestock trampling, and pesticide pollution dries up, it can crumble and blow away, so farmland turns to desert. Desertification threatens 70 percent of Australia's farmland. Sustainable farming and water conservation are vital if agriculture for Australians and for export is to survive into the future.

Ashburton R.

Perth

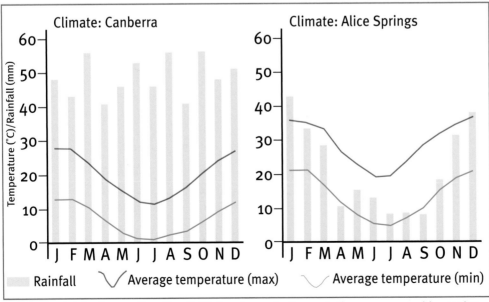

⬆ Coastal Canberra, New South Wales, has rain through the year caused by moist air blown from the ocean, but Alice Springs has a typical arid to desert climate.

N

• Darwin

Artesian wells provide water for sheep, beef cattle and crops in some of Australia's hottest and driest areas.

Great Sandy Desert

Tanami Desert

Northern Territory

• Townsville

Gibson Desert

Little Sandy Desert

•Alice Springs

AUSTRALIA

Queensland

Western Australia

Simpson Desert

Warrego River

Brisbane

South Australia

Lake Eyre North

Barwon River

Great Victoria Desert

Lake Eyre South

Lake Everard

Lake Torrens

Lake Gairdner

Darling River

New South Wales

Lachlan River

Murray River

Murrumbidgee River

• Sydney

• Adelaide

Murray River

• Canberra

• Melbourne

Tasmania

Key

Oil field

Coalfield

Gas field

Areas of desertification

Desert — too dry for farming

See p. 25 for crop and livestock key

0   500 miles

0   1000 km

Now Test Yourself!

These questions will help you to revisit some of the information in this book. To answer the questions, you will need to use the table of contents at the beginning of the book and the index on p. 32, as well as the relevant pages on each topic.

1. Use the table of contents to find which pages show a map of:
   (a) Europe's main fishing areas.
   (b) farming areas in the United States.
   (c) the most southern place on the Earth's surface.

2. Use the index on p. 32 to find the pages that will tell you:
   (a) which parts of the world don't have enough water for people to live in.
   (b) how paper is made from wood.
   (c) how people in Bali can grow rice on steep hillsides.

3. Use the glossary on p. 31 to complete a copy of this table:

Key word	Meaning of this word
	The loss of forest due to chopping down large numbers of trees.
Recycling	
	Rocks that have useful metals in them.
	When people don't have all the water they need.

4. Use p. 6 to find out how long people can survive without any food or water.

5. Use p. 10 to find out what ores are and what they contain.

6. Using pp. 14-15, list any three industrial raw materials and what they are used to make.

7. Use pp. 28-29 to find out which farm animal is raised in very large numbers in Australia.

8. Antarctica is a continent, but the Arctic is not. Use pp 16-17 to find out why.

9. Which regions or countries produces most of the world's:
   (a) diamonds?
   (b) rice?
   (c) tropical hardwoods, such as mahogany?

10. How is the world's increasing population putting pressure on its natural resources?

Glossary

chronic (KRO-nik) Lasting for a long time.

climate change (KLY-mut CHAYNJ) Any long-term significant changes to the weather pattern of a certain area. Climate change can have natural causes, such as volcano eruptions, and is also the result of global warming.

coniferous (kah-NIH-fur-us) An evergreen tree with cones and needlelike leaves.

deciduous (deh-SIH-joo-us) A deciduous tree is one that loses its leaves each year.

deforestation (dee-for-uh-STAY-shun) The loss of forest due to the clearing of large numbers of trees.

desertification (dih-zer-tih-fih-KAY-shun) The word used to describe the spread of the world's deserts.

fertile land (FER-tul LAND) Area with soil that has all the nutrients plants need to grow healthily.

finite resources (FY-nyt REE-sors-ez) Resources which will run out at some time in the future.

fossil fuels (FO-sul FYOOLZ) Sources of energy (like coal, oil, and gas) formed from plants and animals which died millions of years ago.

global warming (GLOH-bul WAWRM-ing) Rising temperatures worldwide, caused by the increase of gases in the air that trap the Sun's heat near Earth.

industrial raw materials (in-DUS-tree-ul RAH muh-TEER-ee-ulz) Natural resources that are used to make goods.

irrigation (ih-rih-GAY-shun) Putting extra water onto the soil because there isn't enough rain to grow crops.

ores (ORZ) Rocks that have useful metals in them.

recycling (ree-SY-kling) When waste materials are used again to make new products.

sustainability (suh-stay-nuh-BIH-lih-tee) Using natural resources in ways which allow people to use them for much longer and cause the least damage to the natural environment.

tropical rain forests (TRAH-puh-kul RAYN FOR-ests) Dense forests which grow in hotter, wetter places nearer to the equator.

water deficit (WAH-ter DEH-fuh-sut) When people don't have all the water they need

water surplus (WAH-ter SUR-plus) When people have more water than they need.

Index

Websites

Due to the changing nature of Internet links, PowerKids Press has developed an online list of websites related to the subject of this book. This site is updated regularly. Please use this link to access the list:

www.powerkidslinks.com/mew/natu/